THE
LITTLE BOOK OF
MAGICKAL
SPELLS

SORAYA

This little book I have prepared,
With knowledge that I wish to share.
May it bring wisdom and bring light,
Whether it be day or night.
Do your work with good intent
That it brings gladness and content.
Never harm another soul
By word or deed or by your goal.
To help another is your aim
By Air and Water, Earth and Flame.

*An it harm none, so mote it be.

*This phrase means "If it harms no-one,
then let it be so".

Caution

The spells in this book often use lit candles. Please never leave a burning candle, or burning incense or charcoal discs, unattended.

The tools to help in your spellcasting may also include sharp objects such as knives for carving symbols. Please take the greatest of care while handling sharp or pointed objects.

Other spell ingredients may include herbs, spices, bark, roots and powders. These ingredients are not intended to be eaten. Please also take care if burning any of these items.

Safe spellcasting!

Blessed be!

Introduction

Witches cast their spells in rhymes and even if you
are an experienced witch you may sometimes find
it difficult to find the right verse for your purpose.
Rhyming gets easier the more often you practise, so
in this book I've provided some magickal verses to
get you started or to be your inspiration. You can use
them as they are or you can modify them to suit your
purpose.

Just remember the golden rules:

* Never try to change another's path.
* When asking for love, never name a specific
  person.
* Never cast a spell asking for money – you never
  know how it may come to you.
* Use your words very carefully as you may get
  what you want but in a manner that will break
  your heart.
* Remain honourable and put others before
  yourself.

'Air I am'

Recite these words over and over again to focus your mind or just to feel good or to connect to your higher power.

These are not my words but are commonly used by witches all over.

Air I am; Fire I am; Water, Earth and Spirit I am.
Air I am; Fire I am; Water, Earth and Spirit I am.
Air I am; Fire I am; Water, Earth and Spirit I am.
Air I am; Fire I am; Water, Earth and Spirit I am.

Casting a Circle

Most rituals take place within a magick or sacred circle. Circles keep energy pure and focused. You yourself should also stay focused. Don't break concentration in the middle of your ceremony, and also try to ensure you are not going to be interrupted. Prepare yourself spiritually and mentally by thinking of your intentions which must always be positive and wholly for the good.

Before you cast any circle, the area that you will be working in should be clean and clear. Here is a short verse that is easy to memorise and can be recited repeatedly while you clean your sacred space. (In fact, you can recite this when you are doing your daily housework!)

I sweep, I sweep my circle clean.
Out with the dirt, and out with the mean.
The energy now is pure and sweet.
My circle now is clean and neat.

Then you may draw your circle:

* Focus your attention on the Lord, Lady or both.

* Draw a circle line from east to north (this can be
  a visualised circle or an actual circle). You may
  well be blessed with enough room in your home
  to draw a circle with a diameter of nine feet (my
  preferred size). In which case, you can stand
  within your circle. If you have very little space,
  please do not worry. Simply visualise that you are
  in a circle. You do not even have to draw it, just
  visualise that you are drawing it. Place the candles
  as described below in the space that you have
  in front of your altar. Then close your eyes and
  imagine a circle forming around you.

* Place a tea light candle at each quarter, beginning at the east and ending at the north.

* Carry a burning incense stick around each of the quarters from the east to the north. This represents the element of Air.

* Light each of the four tea light candles starting at the east. This represents the element of Fire.

* Sprinkle some water around the circle line starting at the east. This represents the element of Water.

* Sprinkle some salt around the perimeter of your circle from the east to the north. This represents the element of Earth.

* Draw a pentacle at each of the four quarters from the east to the north and say a little prayer to ask the guardians of each quarter to guide you in your work. Beginning at the east say: "May the guardian of Air guide and protect me." At the south say: "May the guardian of Fire guide and protect me." At the west say: "May the guardian of Water guide and protect me." At the north say: "May the guardian of Earth guide and protect me."

* Your circle is now ready and you can stand or sit in it.

* Say your prayers to the Lord, Lady or both.

* If you have a magickal intention, such as healing work, making or performing spells, performing rituals, candle or cord magick or creating verses for future use, state it now.

*   When you are ready to close your circle, follow these steps: give thanks to the Lord, Lady or both for listening; move around your circle, starting at the east, snuffing out your candles and thanking each of the quarter guardians (Air, Fire, Water and Earth).

*   When you are finished you need to say something to close your circle such as this:

The circle is now closed
But the work will continue until it is done.
An it harm none, so mote it be.

A Circle Verse for Purity

When you have gathered all your tools and you are about to draw your circle line, here is a verse that you can recite to keep your circle, and those who enter it, pure:

This circle line I now prepare,
Let no-one enter should they dare.
In perfect truth and perfect trust
Let them enter if they must.
This sacred space I dedicate,
Is filled with love and never hate.
We work in peace and harmony,
Blessed by the power of three.
An it harm none, so mote it be.

Crystals

Answers – opal

Career – citrine, tiger's eye

Communication – malachite

Courage – jade, bloodstone

Fertility – moonstone, carnelian

Forgiveness – Apache teardrop

Friendship – moonstone

Good luck – citrine, amber

Gratitude – snow quartz, opal

Harvest – lapis, amber

Health – clear quartz

Home – rhodochrosite

Inspiration – amethyst

Interviews – amethyst, tiger's eye

Love – rose quartz, emerald, sapphire

Marriage – rose quartz

Opportunities – diamond, ruby

Passion – emerald, sapphire

Peace – rhodochrosite

Prosperity – diamond, jade

Protection – turquoise

Secrets – bloodstone, flint

Success – malachite, jade

Travel – turquoise, chrysolite

Victory – bloodstone

Shopping List

Most of the tools and ingredients suggested in this book will be in your home already or can easily be bought in a supermarket. There is no need to go to the considerable expense of purchasing a variety of more unusual items. As time passes and you grow in experience, you will inevitably gather special things to add to your collection of "witchy" accessories. But a good spell will depend on your intention, not on any special tools.

For example, my "boline" that I use daily for inscribing candles and when I am performing magick is an antique letter opener but you could use any knife that you already have in your house. (Once you've used it for magick, try to keep it for that purpose alone.) You will probably already have things like herbs and spices in your kitchen and if not they can easily be purchased, fresh or dried, from normal shops. Crystals can be bought from gift shops and health food stores but you will also find many online sources. No spell

ingredient is ever compulsory. Use your imagination to include things that symbolise your intent. Magick is all about the intention. It is not about what you use – these things are just accessories and although they may help you to focus, it is your intention that is important. Below is a list of things I find very useful to have to hand:

* broom
* knife
* notebook
* salt
* candles, holders, matches
* various herbs and spices
* flameproof dishes
* Tarot cards
* cloths for your altar

* playing cards
* a selection of crystals
* Runes (the symbols painted on stones)
* incense, charcoal discs
* aromatherapy diffusers, oil burners, oils
* coloured pens, pencils or chalks

Rune Symbols

Fehu, **Feoh**: wealth, possessions, earnings

Uruz, **Ur**: strength, potential, energy, courage

Thorn, **Thurisaz**: force, conflict, regeneration

Ansuz, **Ansur**: insight, vision, communication

Rado, **Rad**, **Raidho**: travel, journey, changes

Ken, **Kaunan**: revelation, knowledge, passion

Geofu, **Gebo**: gifts, partnerships, contracts

Wunjo, **Wynn**: joy, pleasure, prosperity

ᚺ   **Hagall, Hagalaz**: destructive forces, wrath

ᚾ   **Nied, Naudiz**: delays, conflict, distress

ᛁ   **Isa, Is**: challenges, grievance, frustration

ᛃ   **Gera, Jera, Jara**: good harvest, peace, hope

ᛇ   **Yr, Iwaz, Eiwaz**: protection, dependability

ᛈ   **Peorth, Perth**: secrets, the future, mysteries

ᛉ   **Eolh, Algiz**: defence, shelter, shield

ᛋ   **Sigel, Sowilo**: success, power, health

Rune Symbols

ᛏ **Teiwaz/Tiwaz**, **Tir**: justice, legal success

ᛒ **Beork**, **Berkanan**: birth, growth, beginnings

ᛖ **Eoh**, **Ehwaz**: a vehicle, harmony, partners

ᛗ **Mann**, **Mannaz**: yourself, society, abilities

ᛚ **Lagu**, **Laguz**: water, fertility, dreams, travel

ᛜ **Ing**, **Ingwaz**: male fertility, family, care

ᛟ **Othel**, **Othala**: property, heritage, community

ᛞ **Dagaz**, **Daeg**: dawn, awakening, clarity

Other Symbols

Eye of Horus – an Egyptian symbol of protection, power and good health.

Yin and Yang – a Chinese symbol of duality and balance; opposite forces are complementary and connected.

Triple Goddess – representing phases of the Moon, this also symbolises the Maiden, the Mother, and the Crone, the separate stages in the female life cycle.

Horned God – the male counterpart of the Triple Goddess, associated with nature, sexuality and the life cycle.

Pentacle – a Wiccan symbol of protection. A magical talisman that is often worn.

Triple Spiral – a pre-Christian Celtic symbol that represents to some Wiccans the concept of the Triple Goddess. Others say it represents the nine-month period of human pregnancy.

Achievement

When you are trying to achieve a goal it is very important to remain focused on your task. Each morning, before you get ready for work, take a few moments to gather your thoughts and look towards the day ahead. Memorise the following verse and recite it each time you are distracted or lose heart — it will help you to stay focused on whatever you are trying to do:

To accomplish is my aim.
Let others plainly see,
That being the best that I can be
Is my philosophy.
I am focused on my goals,
I make progress every day.
For I am blessed by the Lady's love
In each and every way.
An it harm none, so mote it be.

Answers

Decorate your altar with objects that are symbolic of information or calculation such as the High Priest card from the Tarot (face up), the Rune Ansuz, oak leaves, a calculator and nine pens. When you have gathered your tools and everything is in place, cast your circle. When you are ready, stand or sit in front of your altar and recite this verse:

> Questions I have and answers I seek,
> With humility these words I speak.
> Those who seek will surely find.
> Clarity and truth will come to the mind,
> For then I will know what is really true.
> This I believe and hold fast to.
> Through the mist I'll clearly see.
> I ask this of the power of three.
> An it harm none, so mote it be.

Close your circle.

Baby ~ Sleep Safe

There are many ways to say goodnight and tuck your children into bed. This little verse can be recited as you kiss them goodnight:

Precious little child of mine
Go to sleep and wake up fine.
Dream sweet dreams and you will see
That you are blessed by Goddesses three.
The Crone, the Maiden, the Mother too,
Will surely be watching over you.
I say these words, this little charm,
To keep you safe and free from harm.
An it harm none, so mote it be.

Balance

Sometimes we may feel out of sorts and unable to cope with our responsibilities. All we really need at times like this is a little bit of balance in our lives.

You can perform a ritual to help to bring balance and harmony back into your life.

Decorate your altar with objects that are symbolic of balance and harmony. You can use a set of scales (or a photograph of scales), the King of Swords and the Justice Tarot cards (face up), a ruler, four or eight dice and a picture of the Yin and Yang symbol.

When you have gathered your tools and everything is in place, cast your circle.

When you are ready, stand or sit in front of your altar and recite the following verse:

Balance come into my life,
Free me from this inner strife.
Harmony is what I seek,
The reason for these words I speak.
High above me, Lady and Lord,
Heed me please, heed my word.
My day to balance, my path to clear,
Rid me of the state I fear.
I am calm now, see my face,
Blessed in your warm embrace.
An it harm none, so mote it be.

Close your circle.

Banishment

Sometimes in life, we experience situations we would rather avoid. Here is a ritual that you can use to rid yourself of such a situation.

Take a pen and paper and write about the situation that is causing you concern and the reasons why you do not want to be involved in it.

Place a fireproof dish on your altar, along with some matches, the paper you have written on and a tall candle. Keep your altar and the room in which you are working clear of clutter.

When you have gathered your tools and everything is in place, cast your circle.

When you are ready, stand or sit in front of your altar. Light the tall candle, take the paper that describes your situation and light it from the candle. Place it in the fireproof dish and let it burn through while you recite this verse:

There is a certain situation
That gives me grievous agitation.
I seek to banish this bad feeling
And bring instead a time of healing.
I cast away these bad events.
I do this with only pure intent.
No harm to come to anyone,
No grief or pain – it is not done.
An it harm none, so mote it be.

Close your circle.

Beauty

Everyone has a beauty very personal to them, regardless of society's ideas on such things. Casting a spell to look different is a very bad idea but casting a spell to feel different or make the best of yourself is fine.

On these occasions, place a mirror on your altar. Decorate the altar with objects that are symbolic of beauty such as a picture of a work of art that you find beautiful, a figure of Venus, the Tarot Star card (face up) or fresh flowers.

When you have gathered your tools and everything is in place, cast your circle. When you are ready, stand or sit in front of your altar. Hold your hands up, palms towards your face, and cross your hands so that your wrists are touching each other. In that position raise your arms so that your crossed wrists are just above your forehead. Your fingers should be splayed open. Now draw your hands down over

your face and visualise that you are becoming more beautiful. Draw your hands out to separate them then go back to the beginning and repeat this exercise. Do this several times while reciting the following verse:

Mirror, mirror on the wall,
I ask the Lady to come to call.
Beauty is my heart's desire,
Blessed by Water, Earth, Air and Fire.
To look my best is what I seek,
Yet I remain humble and meek.
'Tis not in ego I seek to gain,
But more confidence I must obtain.
I ask this of the Goddesses three,
An it harm none, so mote it be.

Close your circle.

Beltane

Beltane is a Pagan festival held on April 30th or May 1st every year to mark the beginning of summer. It's a Fire festival and a time to celebrate the joy of love and fertility and the union of the Goddess and the God.

To celebrate this festival begin by decorating your altar with summer fruits and flowers and photographs of loving couples and happy holidays.

When you have gathered your tools and everything is in place, cast your circle.

When you are ready, stand or sit in front of your altar and recite the following verse:

Beltane blessings to one and all.
I hear the voice of summer call,
Summer rain or summer sun,
Now's the time to have some fun.
Laughter in the air I hear,
For 'tis the time of summer cheer.
The Lady dances with her Lord
As music plays a happy chord.
We celebrate this time and share,
And show our loved ones that we care.
Lord and Lady we follow thee.
An it harm none, so mote it be.

Close your circle.

Book of Shadows

A Book of Shadows is a very personal notebook. Witches keep their favourite spells and rituals written in it. When you receive your first Book of Shadows, the chances are that you won't know what to put in it first. Almost everyone experiences this common problem. Here is a ritual verse that can be the first thing to go into your book and, what's more, you can perform this ritual to bless your book when you begin your journey on the path of the Wise.

Place your Book of Shadows in the centre of your altar. Decorate your altar with some candles, a pentacle (or a picture of one) and some flowers to make it pretty. If you have Tarot cards, you can place The Magician card face up on your altar to symbolise the beginning of your journey.

When you have gathered your tools and everything is in place, cast your circle. When you are ready, stand or sit in front of your altar and recite the following verse:

This book of mine I dedicate
To spells and rituals that I create,
To all the things that I will learn,
To all the experience that I earn.
On its pages I will describe
My journey and my secrets scribe.
My grimoire it will blessed-be
From above by the power of three.
I will be inspired each time I look
Into my blessed, sacred book.
An it harm none, so mote it be.

Close your circle.

Break a Curse

Have you ever had the feeling that someone has cursed you? I hope not but if you ever do here is a spell to break a curse.

Start by finding an old cup or plate that you don't mind doing without (during the ritual you will break it). Place the plate or cup on your altar along with a hammer and a cloth bag or a pillowcase. The surface of your altar should be free from clutter but if you feel the need you can add items that are symbolic of flight such as a picture of a bird or a dragon. These items will add power to your intention.

When you have gathered your tools and everything is in place, cast your circle. When you are ready, stand in front of your altar and recite the following verse as you place the cup or plate in the cloth bag or pillowcase and carefully break it once with the hammer, then once more, and finally a third time:

I break the curse that came to me,
That I be well for all to see.
I send it back from whence it came,
The bidder takes back all the pain.
I am free from any blight,
My life is filled with love and light.
The threefold rule it does protect,
The Goddess's laws we must respect.
We bide this rule — see no-one harmed —
The curse returned and sender warned.
Be mindful of whatever you send,
It will come back and you will bend.
An it harm none, so mote it be.

Close your circle.

Break a Spell

I once cast a spell for love.

This was a spontaneous moment that I followed without thinking of the consequences of my action. I did draw love towards me. The person loved me but sadly I did not share that love. The damage was already done before I realised and it was too late to break the spell.

Here is a way for you to break a thoughtless spell, providing you recognise your mistake quickly.

Keep your altar clear and uncluttered. When you have gathered all your tools and everything is in place, cast your circle.

When you are ready, stand or sit in front of your altar and recite the following verse:

A spell I made without good thought,
Let the wake of this please come to naught.
Lord and Lady hear my plea,
Break this spell I ask of thee.
My words, though wrong, no harm was meant,
Thoughtless gain was my intent.
See my error and break it please.
An it harm none, so mote it be.

Close your circle.

Broken Bones

Broken bones need time to heal properly. Doing a spell to heal them quickly is not recommended because you could cause them to heal when they are not fully aligned. To avoid this, simply perform your spell with the intention of removing or reducing the pain of the person who has suffered the injury.

Accessories to decorate your altar can include things like chamomile flowers (wonderful for healing and easing pain) and two readily available crystals, malachite (particularly good for fractures) and tiger's eye (better for breaks). Either of these crystals can be placed on your altar and/or given to the person who has been injured. I know someone who tucked a crystal into the top of their cast.

When you have gathered your tools and everything is in place, cast your circle. When you are ready, stand or sit in front of your altar and recite the following verse:

Your broken bone it pains you sore,
Let it not pain you any more.
I send you light to bring you ease,
The Goddess listens to our pleas.
Be well, be strong, and heal in time.
Let nature help you, let body be fine.
The doctors tending you will find
That you are strong in body and mind.
With kindest will my love is sent,
For you to get well is our intent.
The Lady listens to our plea,
An it harm none, so mote it be.

Close your circle.

Cleansing a New Broomstick

Every witch needs a broom! A broom is used for clearing areas for ritual work. You can buy a broom from your local hardware store and decorate it by carving Rune symbols or planet glyphs into the broomstick. Dress it with coloured feathers and beads to personalise it and make it your own. Your new broom is now ready to be cleansed using the following ritual.

Place your decorated broom on your altar together with a small dish of water and some salt. When you have gathered your tools and everything is in place, cast your circle. When you are ready, add three pinches of salt to the water in the dish, placing the point of your index finger in the water as you add the salt and repeating these words:

> Salt is life, here is life, blessed be without strife.
> Salt is life, here is life, blessed be without strife.
> Salt is life, here is life, blessed be without strife.

Now sprinkle the consecrated water over your broom and say:

> I bless this broom, to cleanse it sure,
> To keep my space both safe and pure.
> It guards my home, it guards my hearth,
> It brushes clean the sacred Earth.
> Others know the work I do,
> And my broom it shows this too.
> When they see it against the wall,
> They know it is good for them to call.
> When I am working, it will be,
> In my circle helping me.
> With Air and Water, Fire and Earth,
> My broom is sacred to my hearth.
> An it harm none, so mote it be.

Close your circle.

Business ~ New

When you or someone you care for is about to start a new business, this spell will empower your or their efforts.

Decorate your altar with objects that depict new opportunities or new beginnings. The following Tarot cards can be placed face up on your altar: the Magician (symbolising a new beginning), the Empress (symbolising growth) and the King and Queen of Pentacles (symbolising material abundance).

When you have gathered your tools and everything is in place, cast your circle.

When you are ready, stand or sit in front of your altar and recite this verse:

To start a business is our quest,
Our results are going to be the best.
We expect a good response,
Ready we are to take a chance.
Please, Luna Lady hear this plea,
And bless us by the power of three,
The Maiden, Mother and the Crone.
Your blessing to us you oft have shown,
And now we ask this wish of thee,
An it harm none, so mote it be.

Close your circle.

Business Success ~ 1

A good way to watch this spell grow is by using a flowerpot, some soil and some seeds. The best time of year to perform this ritual spell is between spring and summer, when it's easier to grow things. For planting later in the year use bulbs such as hyacinths, snowdrops, crocuses or daffodils. Of course, all this depends on where you live and the weather.

Once you have decided on the right plant for the time of year, decorate your altar with objects that are symbolic of growth such as a packet of yeast, a money plant (also called the jade plant) and some citrine crystals (citrine is also known as the Merchant's Stone). Place a flowerpot, some pebbles, some soil, seeds (or bulbs), a piece of paper and a pencil on your altar.

When you have gathered your tools together and everything is in place, cast your circle. When you are ready, write the verse that follows on the piece of

paper and place it in the bottom of the flowerpot. Add a few pebbles for drainage, some soil and then some seeds (or bulbs) on top. Cover with soil and water carefully.

When this is done, recite this verse:

> This work I do, I do it well,
> My aim is to succeed.
> So here and now I ask the Lord,
> That my business be like a seed,
> That it grow strong and bear good fruit
> Just like the Lady doth.
> I give my word I will work hard,
> Of this I give my oath.
> An it harm none, so mote it be.

Close your circle.

Business Success ~ 2

Once your business is established, the following spell will help it to grow and succeed.

This time, decorate your altar with things that are synonymous with success such as items made of gold or silver, photographs of expensive cars or anything else that means success to you in your field. You can add the Wheel and the Star Tarot cards (face up).

When you have gathered your tools and everything is in place, cast your circle.

When you are ready, stand or sit in front of your altar and recite the following verse:

Our business reputation grows.
Progress, time and profit shows.
Customers to us are drawn
By efficiency and a welcome warm.
We do succeed in all we do,
With effort, skill and kindness too.
Our lives are blessed for all to see,
These wishes come from the power of three.
An it harm none, so mote it be.

Close your circle.

Calmness for Yourself

Take a few deep meditative breaths before you begin
this spell. Place items on your altar that to you
symbolise peace, quiet and calm such as a picture of
a peaceful scene, a book of poetry or maybe an object
from a pastime that distracts you from a hectic life.
You can use the following verse without casting a
circle if you are at work or in a stressful place, but, if
you can and for the full effect, cast your circle in the
usual way. When you are ready, recite this verse:

> Restore calm to my hectic life,
> Banish chaos, fear and strife.
> Peace reigns again and I feel fine,
> Stillness, quiet and calm is mine.
> An it harm none, so mote it be.

Close your circle. (To calm yourself even more, you
could also take a purifying bath as described on
pages 165–6.)

Calmness For Another

The following verse can be written in a card or letter and sent to whoever needs some words of comfort or support:

Be calm, be still, banish hurt and fear,
The Lady listens to my plea.
She helps to ease your burden and she hears
This blessing sent to you from me.
She enfolds you in her love,
With blessings sent from high above.
An it harm none, so mote it be.

Career ~ A Change

There is more to creating magick than just casting circles and reciting verses. You also have to play an active part when it comes to making spells for your own benefit. In this case it means you have to be doing everything you can to find the right job for you. If you do not put any effort into this, neither will the Lord nor Lady.

When it comes to asking for a change of career, don't wish for a particular job. You might get what you asked for only to discover it is nothing like you thought it was going to be. This career spell asks for some of the things that make any job enjoyable.

Prepare your altar by placing the following Tarot cards face up on your altar: the Judgement card (new beginnings), the High Priest card (knowledge), the Ace of Swords card (empowerment) and the Ace of Wands card (inspiration). You can also use the Rune symbol Tir (sometimes known as Teiwaz depicting the spiritual warrior and courage) on your altar.

When you have gathered your tools and everything is in place, cast your circle. When you are ready, stand or sit in front of your altar and recite this verse:

A change I need, in my career,
Rewarding work, done without fear,
With workmates friendly and effective,
Who can see things from my perspective.
This change will bring me some reward,
For over the years I have worked hard.
Blessed are the Ladies three,
Maiden, Mother and Crone are they.
This is my wish, this is my plea.
An it harm none, so mote it be.

Close your circle.

Career ~ Interview

If your job searching and spell casting are successful you may need guidance for an interview.

If you want to perform the ritual for another person it can be easily adapted, but do ask them first! Don't cast a spell for someone who doesn't want it.

Prepare your altar. You can use the same objects to decorate your altar as suggested in the previous spell.

When you have gathered your tools together and everything is in place, cast your circle.

When you are ready, stand or sit in front of your altar and recite the verse opposite:

An interview I must attend
To be the best I do intend.
Against all others I will be
The best match as an employee.
My skills are there, my knowledge too,
Experience – I have that too.
This job is mine if the time is right,
I wish this now with all my might.
But if this job is not for me
Then a better one will surely be.
What's for the best the Lady can see.
An it harm none, so mote it be.

Close your circle.

Career ~ Promotion

This spell is for those who are seeking to be better rewarded for their efforts at work – in other words, a spell asking for promotion.

As with any other spell it is important that you remember to add the words "An it harm none, so mote it be". By doing so you will ensure that your spell creates the right situation for you without interfering with another's destiny or true path.

Prepare your altar with things that are typical of the tools you use in your work and will use in the position that you desire.

Gather your tools together and when everything is in place, cast your circle. When you are ready, stand or sit in front of your altar and recite the following verse:

A promotion now is what I seek.
My abilities are at their peak.
If this is the right time for me,
Then let me be an interviewee.
I am worth a better post.
I can manage more than most.
A role that gives me better reward
Because I have been working hard.
A role that uses all my skills,
A role that my potential fulfils.
These seeds of hope I sow
That they may thrive,
And may my prayers come alive.
An it harm none, so mote it be.

Close your circle.

Career ~ Success

Decorate your altar with objects that are symbolic of information or calculation such as the High Priest card from the Tarot (lay it down face up), the Rune symbol Ansuz, some leaves from an oak tree, a calculator, and nine pencils, pens or pieces of chalk. These items will add power to your intention.

When you have gathered your tools together and everything is in place, cast your circle.

When you are ready, stand or sit in front of your altar and recite the verse opposite:

Is that my name I hear them cry?
No longer do they pass me by.
Instead, they come right to my door,
For my help, advice and more.
My work revered, my talent too,
All with thanks and love to you.
Fulfilled and happy, I can see
That I am blessed by the power of three.
An it harm none, so mote it be.

Close your circle.

Caution

There may be times in your life when you have to have to deal with a dangerous situation or a person who is quick to anger. In cases like these, you need to use caution in what you say and do. This is not always an easy thing to do. Here is something that will help you to remain cautious.

Breathe deeply and slowly and visualise a beautiful rose. Imagine that you want to pick that rose but you can see that it has very sharp thorns. Recognise that you cannot just reach out and grasp the rose because, if you do, the thorns will prick your hands. Recognise that you have to use caution and handle this rose carefully. Take your time. See where the thorns are and where the gaps are so that you can pick the rose up safely. Perform this exercise frequently. When you are face to face with a difficult situation or person, imagine that you see a rose in front of that person or situation and this should help you to be cautious.

If you prefer to perform a ritual, decorate your altar with objects that are sharp such as a thorny rose stem or a piece of broken glass. You can also use the Rune symbol for Thurizas and a bunch of sage. Gather your tools and when everything is in place, cast your circle. When you are ready, stand or sit in front of your altar and recite this verse:

> Sharp edges tell me that I'm warned.
> Caution will see that I'm not harmed.
> A prickly person or situation,
> Need not cause such agitation.
> Take your anger and opposition,
> And think on it with real contrition.
> Lord and Lady make me cautious
> In these dealings, angry and thoughtless.
> Keep me in your safe embrace,
> When I meet this risk I face.
> An it harm none, so mote it be.

Close your circle.

Clarity

It can be difficult to solve a problem when you cannot see clearly what the cause is. What you need is clarity.

Place a candle in the centre of your altar and place a piece of glass in front of the candle so that you have to look through the glass to see the candle. Place nothing else on your altar. Keep it completely bare.

When you have gathered your tools together and everything is in place, cast your circle .

When you are ready, light your altar candle, then sit in front of your altar.

Recite the the verse on the next page repeatedly for a while, then spend some quiet time gazing at the candle through the glass.

While you are gazing at the candle, think about the problem you wish to solve. When you are done, you should have a greater understanding of its cause and how to solve it.

Help me Goddess, let me know,
That I may understand anew,
What the answers here might be
To this problem worrying me.
I will see clearly, when She speaks
And listen for the words I seek.
I'll understand, for I can see,
And I am blessed by the power of three.
An it harm none, so mote it be.

Close your circle.

Communication

How many times have you heard or said, "You are not listening to me"? In Native American tradition, when two or more people converse, each one can speak without interruption as long as they are holding a "talking stick". When they are finished what they have to say, they pass the stick to the next person. This allows others in the conversation to listen carefully to what is being said before it is their turn to speak without interruption.

What is it that you find difficult when it comes to communicating with other people? Are you worried about speaking in public or in a group? Do you find it hard to talk to a specific person or about a specific subject? Reciting the verse on the next page will help you whenever you are struggling to find the right words.

You can also use this verse in the following ritual to improve your communication skills. Before you

begin, think about what you want to say and how you want to get your point across. Write down what you want to say on a piece of paper and place it on your altar. When you have gathered your tools and everything is in place, cast your circle. Stand or sit in front of your altar and recite this verse:

No spite or anger will I use,
To speak the words that I peruse.
Ensuring that my point is clear,
That others listen and can hear.
Whatever it is I have to write,
Put pen to paper, then speak with might.
Let my words be clear and clean,
Never angry, never mean.
I ask this of the Witches three,
An it harm none, so mote it be.

Close your circle.

Communication

Many things can distract us when we are trying to perform a new task or learn something new. One of the best ways of learning how to concentrate is by practising meditation.
Sit on a chair or cross-legged on the floor — whatever you find most comfortable — and relax. Breathe deeply and slowly.

Visualise a symbol of the subject you want to study or use a physical symbolic object and place it so that it is at eye level as you sit before it in your meditation position. Gaze at the object (real or imagined) and take in every detail. Try not to think of the object in words, just take it in visually. You might find your mind wandering but draw it back to concentrate on your object or symbol. Practise this regularly to improve your concentration.

You can also learn the following verse off by heart and when faced with a new challenge that demands your concentration repeat the verse several times within a mental circle:

I am focused on my task,
And nothing will distract me.
Clear in mind I am at last,
No other thoughts will find me.
My thoughts are clear, my words are too,
Of that I can be sure.
And when I write or speak anew,
The message will be pure.
An it harm none, so mote it be.

Close your circle.

Confidence

On your altar, place items that are symbolic of knowledge such as "how-to" books, a dictionary and the Rune symbol Ansuz. You can also lay a sprig of sage on your altar and burn some clary sage essential oil in an oil burner. When you are ready, cast your circle. Stand or sit in front of your altar and recite this verse:

> Sure and confident I can be,
> A gift from the Lady, one, two, three.
> My head held high, my steps are sure,
> My words ring true, my words are pure.
> "Be not afraid," the Lady says,
> "Be confident in all your days,
> "Be wise, be steady, and be assured,
> "Your confident nature is secured."
> This is my wish, this is my plea,
> An it harm none, so mote it be.

Close your circle.

Courage

Decorate your altar with some jade, bloodstone or malachite crystals (stones in the breastplates of warriors going into battle); one red candle (passion), one white candle (the spiritual warrior), the Rune symbol Teiwaz and the Tarot card Strength (face up). Cast your circle. Light the candles then raise your hands high above your head and say these words:

> Courage and strength I possess,
> Given to me by the great God Bes.
> The God Samael blesses me,
> Brave I am, and all can see.
> A challenge I may face once more,
> Like many have I faced before.
> Prepared I am to face this task,
> Courage my prayer – courage I ask.
> The Lord and Lady, they bless me,
> An it harm none, so mote it be.

Close your circle.

Craft Work ~ To Sell

Many people nowadays are using their creative skills and selling their craft work online and at fairs. When you are selling your goods at craft fairs, imagine yourself surrounded by bright, heavenly light and keep away negative energies such as envy.

You can cast a circle in a public place by visualising it. Remember to leave a doorway open in the space in front of your table so that your customers can come and go.

Write the verse opposite on a piece of paper and place it face up on your table but under a cloth so that it cannot be seen by others.

You will know it is there and that is what matters. From time to time throughout the day, mentally recite the verse to keep the energy flowing:

The door is open for those to come,
Who wish to see what we have done.
To sell our work is our intention,
Let people give us their attention.
This is our craft, this is our skill,
These gifts you give us by your will.
What we create let others see,
We ask your blessings by the power of three.
An it harm none, so mote it be.

Creativity

Since your skills are given to you by your Creator, it is an act of respect to cast a circle wherever you are working. Doing this will inspire you and help your creative juices to flow.

All your craft tools are symbolic of what you are doing and your craft surface becomes your altar. Three is the number of fertility and growth, so group your tools in threes on your altar to empower your creative energy. You can also decorate your altar with objects that are symbolic of growth such as the Empress Tarot card (face up) and the Rune symbol Beork (sometimes known as Berkana).

When everything is in place, cast a circle. (You can create a real circle or, if circumstances dictate it, simply visualise your circle.)

When you are ready, recite the following verse:

May the Goddess up above,
Bless my tools with light and love.
May they create work that is true,
With wisdom, insight and knowledge too.
Goddess be my inspiration
With talent, truth and innovation.
An it harm none, so mote it be.

Close your circle.

You can also write the verse above (or a verse of your own) on a piece of paper, put it in a frame and keep it on your work surface. Whenever you begin to lose focus, you can recite the verse.

Crystal Cleansing

Crystals empower your intentions in a spell. They are often used to decorate your altar. There is a short list of crystals and what they stand for on page 13. When you first buy a crystal, it should be cleansed. The simplest of way of doing this is to wash it in running water. Once cleansed, you can dedicate it to any purpose. To dedicate a crystal, hold it in your hand and think about the purpose that you wish it to have. Here is a simple verse with which you can bless your crystal:

Little crystal pure and bright,
Feel my love for you this night,
Work with me to achieve my task,
This is all of you I ask.
For good my purpose will always be,
Blessed by the power of three.
Let no harm come to you or me,
An it harm none, so mote it be.

Deadlines

If you are under pressure, there is no point in suggesting that you cast a circle and do a ritual because you probably feel that you do not have the time. However, a moment or two given to doing this will relax and calm you and probably make you work more competently. Cast a simple mental circle, light a candle and stand quietly for a moment to compose yourself. When you are ready, take a deep breath, relax and recite the following verse:

Under pressure I may be,
As demands are made of me.
But – no matter – I will cope,
For there is always blessed hope.
The Lady sees my struggle too,
And she blesses me anew,
That I can cope with life's demands.
The power to meet them is in my hands,
An it harm none, so mote it be.

Deadlock

If you are ever in a situation where agreement cannot be reached, here is a simple spell that you can perform to break the deadlock. Gather a pair of scissors, several pieces of string and a fireproof dish. Place these on your altar. Cast a circle. Recite the following verse as you take the scissors and cut through each piece of string.

He says "yes" and I say "no".
Our progress here is very slow.
On a topic we cannot agree.
The other's side we cannot see.
And so it goes, around and around,
That the solution cannot be found.
But Lord of mercy set us free,
Help us finally to agree.
An it harm none, so mote it be.

When you are done, place the pieces of string into the fireproof dish and set them alight. Close your circle.

Deceit

Sometimes when we are listening to someone, our instincts may tell us that they are lying. We may accept what they are saying but in our hearts we know it's a lie. Although the truth may be hard to accept, it will always help you to see clearly. Place a white candle in the centre of your altar to represent purity and truth. Cast a circle. To banish deceit, light the white candle and recite this verse:

> Deceitful I will never be,
> Lying, it is not for me.
> I speak the truth and so must he/she,
> For then we will all be set free.
> Free from hurt and lack of trust,
> This can be done, it is a must.
> Lady help us in our task,
> That we be truthful till the last.
> An it harm none, so mote it be.

Close your circle.

Decisions

It can be difficult to make a choice or take a decision until you have all the information that you need. Always trust your instincts because they will guide you but if you are still unsure try the following ritual.

Place a piece of paper and a pen on your altar together with a candle and the Judgement card from a Tarot deck on your altar (face up). When your tools are all gathered and everything is in place, cast a circle. When you are ready, light the altar candle and pick up the Judgement card. Sit quietly in front of your altar and gaze at the Judgement card. After a while, your attention may drift to the candle flame. Allow that to happen and quietly think about the choice or decision that you are trying to make. Next take the piece of paper and the pen and write down all the positive aspects of each choice. Now write down all the negative aspects. Now calculate the effect that the positive aspects would have on your life. Do the same

for the negative aspects. Try to come to a decision after weighing up the pros and cons of each choice. Work on this until you are tired. If necessary take a break and then go back to your circle and stand or sit in front of your altar with your arms raised high over your head and recite the verse below:

Is it yes or is it no?
How to know which way to go?
Am I wrong or am I right?
Lady can you hear my plight?
I now see the way to go.
Sure I am, and now I know
How to make the choice, you see.
For I am blessed by the power of three.
An it harm none, so mote it be.

Do this from beginning to end until you have made your choice. Close the circle.

Dedication

The festival of Imbolc (February 1st or 2nd) marks the beginning of Spring. It is the perfect time to dedicate yourself or re-affirm your vows to follow the "path of the Wise". With Spring approaching, the colours yellow and gold are significant. Use these colours to decorate your altar and make it as bright and pretty as you can. Place two candles on your altar for balance as well as a pentacle or a picture of one.

Treat this occasion as you would were it a Christening or a formal ceremony for those who are about to make a vow. Have a bath or a shower, fix your hair and think about your intentions.

When you have gathered your tools and everything is in place, cast your circle. When you are ready, light the altar candles and recite the following verse:

The Wiccan path it is for me,
The Goddess guides my way.
Whether it be hard or trouble-free,
"I am a Witch," I say.
The thricefold law rules how I act.
I think of others, this is my pact.
To do my best, this is my vow,
I walk the Wiccan path from now.
The Goddess helps me do what's right
And knows what's best for me.
Each morning, noon and every night,
This is my vow, so mote it be.

Close your circle.

Divination with Crystals

This is a spell to tell the future. For any kind of divination, your mind must be clear and your heart pure. Do not allow any distractions, worries or anxieties to influence you.

Choose the crystals that you want to use or make a random selection and place these on your altar. Decorate your altar with as little as possible. One candle and a pentacle are more than enough for this ritual.

When you have gathered your tools and everything is in place, cast a circle.

When you are ready, stand or sit in front of your altar. Light the altar candle and look at the crystals. Look at the shape they have formed, their colours and the number of crystals and make a mental note of what these things mean to you.

Recite the following verse:

> Crystals pure and oh so bright,
> Bless me now with your insight.
> Show me now what I should know,
> Lead me now and I will follow.
> By shape or colour I can see
> What you are showing now to me.
> Lead me, guide me, show me true,
> That I know best what I should do.
> An it harm none, so mote it be.

Close your circle.

Keep a note of your impressions in your Book of Shadows and refer to it in the future to see if you have been accurate.

Drawing Down the Moon

"Drawing Down the Moon" is a ritual performed to fill yourself with divine light or the essence of the Goddess. Any woman or man can perform it. It can help to heal, bring strength and empower you. You must stand outside on a moonlit night when the Moon is full and bright. (It is best done when the Moon is full but can be done anytime.)

You can choose to visualise a circle around you. See yourself enclosed in the glow of sparkling white energy. Raise your eyes, gaze at the Moon and breathe slowly and deeply before beginning to recite the verse that follows on pages 86–87. If you are unobserved, you can raise your arms high above your head as you recite the verse but, if this is not possible, simply stand with your arms by your sides.

This ceremony is best performed, however, outdoors in a full ritual. Start by decorating your altar with white or silver objects and candles to represent the Goddess.

To cast your circle, focus your attention on the Goddess and draw your circle line from east to north.

Place a tea light candle at each quarter, beginning at the east and ending at the north. Light an incense stick and carry it around your circle from the east to the north. Return to the east and light each of the four tea light candles in turn.

Put three pinches of salt in a small dish of water and sprinkle this around the circle line starting at the east.

Draw a pentacle at each of the four quarters from the east to the north and say a little prayer to ask the guardians of each quarter (Air, Fire, Water and Earth) to guide you in your work. You can say something simple such as "May the guardian of Air/Fire/Water/Earth guide and protect me."

When you are ready, stand in front of your altar and recite the verse on the next two pages.

Luna Lady, high above,
Come bless me now with light and love.
Hear my prayer at full of moon.
Come to me now, come to me soon.
She who lives within our kind,
Bless our body, heart and mind.
Welcome here into my space,
Let me gaze upon your face.
Lady I have known your name,
Yet your purpose stays the same.
Mother, Maiden, and Crone too,
Empower me now to feel anew.

Feel the love I give to you,
Feel my worship, pure and true.
This I promise on this night,
You are all my love, my light.
Keep me safe and free from harm,
Bless me now with all your charm.
I've known you many times before,
May I know you many more.
Let me be as one with you,
Loved and blessed, loved and pure.
I am She who gives all life
I am She this full Moon night.
An it harm none, so mote it be.

Embarrassment

Blushing, when you see it in another person, can be very attractive but if you are the one who is blushing it can be an embarrassing experience, especially if anyone comments on the fact – which makes you blush even more!

Most people grow out of blushing but for some it remains an affliction well into adulthood. If you suffer from this, the verse opposite may help you.

There is no need to cast a circle, just memorise and recite the verse whenever you can. If you are going to be in a stressful situation where you fear embarrassment or feel self-conscious then say it before the event and recite it to yourself during the event.

If my face reveals I'm timid,
A blush appears, red and vivid.
Lady let me find the nerve,
And confidence in my reserves.

As others are, let me be seen,
Not red of face, but quite serene.
My embarrassment it does not show,
I smile and let my beauty glow.
An it harm none, so mote it be.

Close your circle.

Employment

Being unemployed is not a pleasant experience but there are some things you can do that will hurry destiny along and help you to find work (also take a look at the "Career" spells on pages 52–59).

First decorate your altar with the High Priest Tarot card, a set of keys (representing new doors opening), job vacancies cut from current newspapers (of a type that you would like to do) and a piece of paper on which you have written a list of your skills and experience.

When you have gathered all your tools and everything is in place, cast a circle.

When you are ready, stand or sit in front of your altar and recite the verse on the next page.

Gainful work is what I need.
To the Lady's will I do concede.
I need to work, and so I trust
The Goddess – help me earn a crust.
Goddess bless me with employment,
This is my wish 'tis my intent.
A quick solution is desired,
So I can pay what is required.
An it harm none, so mote it be.

Close your circle.

After that, place your list in a frame and put a silver coin under the glass inside the frame. Sit the frame in a private place where it will not be seen by random visitors. Place a tea light candle in front of your frame. Light your candle every day and recite the verse above while doing so.

Education

Embarking on a path of education can be a daunting task regardless of your age or experience.

This verse will help you on your journey and it can be recited whenever you need it:

> I wish to study and to learn,
> That knowledge I may gain.
> For it's my wish to now accrue,
> The wisdom I can learn anew.
> I ask the Lady show me the way,
> That I may learn more every day.
> Guide me on my path true,
> This is the prayer I ask of you.
> This is my wish, oh let it be
> Blessed by the power of three.
> An it harm none, so mote it be.

Family

This is a spell to keep your family safe from harm. Decorate your altar with objects that are symbolic of a happy family such as photographs of your own family in happy times or other pictures that symbolise happy family life. The Rune symbols Algiz (protection) and Othel (the home) can be used on your altar as can the Empress Tarot card (Mother figure). Set candles on either side of your photographs. When everything is in place, cast your circle. Now light the altar candles and recite the following verse:

> My family, let them blessed be,
> Enfolded in the arms of three,
> The Maiden, Mother and the Crone,
> Ensure that they are safe and warm.
> I say this prayer every day,
> To keep them safe in every way,
> An it harm none, so mote it be.

Close your circle.

Family

This is a spell that asks the Goddess to make a woman more fertile in order to have a child of her own. The best time of the year for this spell is around the first day of May when the Maiden meets her God, they fall in love, mate and she becomes with child.

For this spell, there are several objects that you can use to decorate your altar. The first is a poppy whose delicate red petals depict the womb. You can use a real flower or, if they are not in season, you can use a photograph. Frogs and rabbits also symbolise fertility, as do eggs and fruits such as pomegranates and figs.

When you have gathered your tools and everything is in place, cast your circle. Stand or sit in front of your altar and recite the following verse:

At this time my dearest wish
Is a child to call my own.
With the Goddess's love and blessing,
As a mother I'll be known.
I ask the Goddess grant my plea
And bless me with fertility.
An it harm none, so mote it be.

Close your circle.

The following can also encourage fertility: carrying, whenever possible, moonstone crystals (blessed with the power to heal women's menstrual cycles) and the Rune symbol Berkana (also called Beork and depicting a new life or the birth of a child); reciting the verse above daily; and following a healthy, proper diet in order to prepare the body for pregnancy.

Forgiveness

Sometimes it is very hard to forgive someone when you feel offended or hurt in some way. To find forgiveness in your heart or to be forgiven by another person, you need to understand the circumstances behind the events that caused the hurt.

To do this place a candle in front of you. Light it and hold the Six of Cups Tarot card in the palms of your hands.

The Six of Cups is a very karmic card and deals with past issues. The best Tarot deck to use for this ritual is the traditional Rider Waite deck as the illustrations in other Tarot decks may not be as helpful as those in the Rider Waite deck.

You should be sitting comfortably with your hands resting on your knees so that you can see the card clearly. Take a few deep relaxing breaths and focus your attention on the card.

Keep your attention on the card for several minutes and then reflect on the circumstances behind the events that require forgiveness. Continue to look at the Six of Cups while you do this.

Every time you reach a point where you feel as though you cannot forgive or will not be forgiven, take a few deep calming breaths and start again. Do not be surprised if you cry – this is part of the process.

You can use the following verse for both forgiving and being forgiven (changing "forgiveness" to "sorry"):

> Zeus and Hera hear me pray,
> Hurts and wrongs are now forgiven.
> Forgiveness/Sorry is the word I say,
> Love restored, my joy has risen,
> An it harm none, so be it.

Freedom

To be released from any kind of restriction, gather together some strands of wool or string and a pair of scissors. Place them on your altar. Keep your altar simple and free from any clutter for this spell.

When you have gathered your tools and everything is in place, cast your circle.

When you are ready, sit in front of your altar, take three strands of wool or string and bind them into a plait. Do this until you have at least three completed plaits.

Tie these plaits round your non-dominant wrist and then take up the scissors and one by one cut through the plaits while you recite this verse:

Release me from the ties that bind,
For you are loving, you are kind.
Set me free from misery,
Set me free and let me be.
An it harm none, so mote it be.

Close your circle.

Friendship

Magick is not just about casting spells. You must use the gifts you have been given by the Goddess. Remember that in order to make friends you must be pro-active and put yourself in situations where you have to interact with people. You cannot ask for a specific person to become your friend because you cannot interfere with another person's will but you can ask for friendship in general to come to you, as in the following verse:

> In recent days I've I felt alone,
> And long to make more friends of my own.
> A true and good friend I will prove,
> If my shyness I can remove.
> Let me meet people who are kind,
> Trustworthy and of like mind.
> Goddess hear my heartfelt plea.
> An it harm none, so mote it be.

Friendship ~ Gratitude

This is a verse in gratitude for friendship that can be written in a greetings card or a letter. It can also be recited in a circle if time allows.

Our friends may come and they may go,
But always they will be,
Close to our hearts and in our thoughts,
Wherever they may be.
They have no doubts, they always know,
Our love it crosses land and sea.
Our friendship travels where they go,
And lasts eternally.
I give my gratitude for them,
My Lady from above,
Success to them in all they do,
And blessings of light and love.
An it harm none, so mote it be.

Goddess Verse

Invoking the Goddess is a powerful thing to do
for all your spell work. Decorate your altar with
depictions of the Goddess in all her forms: Maiden,
Mother and Crone. You could also use the Triple
Goddess symbol or the Triple Spiral symbol (see
pages 19–20), white and silver candles and any
objects depicting moons and stars. Cast your circle.
Stand or sit in front of your altar and recite this
verse:

> I sing to the Goddess, I sing "blessed be".
> I invoke the Goddess by the power of three.
> The Maiden, the Mother, the old Crone, I call,
> I worship and honour her one and all.
> Come to me, come to me, come to me now.
> Come to me, hear me, for I make a vow,
> To love and respect thee where e'er I may be,
> This is my vow to the Goddesses three.
> An it harm none, so mote it be.

Close your circle.

Goodbye

This is a verse that could be for a friend who is moving to a new location, maybe because of a new job.

A simple way to offer this verse to a friend is to copy the words into a card or a letter and give it to them, either by post or personally.

I wish you well in all you do,
This blessing comes from me to you,
As you are off to pastures new.
May your success continue through
Your hard-earned skills and talents true.
Blessed be loved ones and new friends too.
I ask this by the power of three,
An it harm none, so mote it be.

Good Humour

On those days when you feel like you can't shift an irritable mood think of this little spell. You don't need to cast a circle, just repeat the verse below to yourself and imagine that dark cloud of irritability drifting away and being replaced by the blue skies of a good mood.

This will be more effective if you also concentrate on the positive things that have happened in your day, no matter how minor.

Cast off this cloud above my head
And bring some laughs to me instead.
Lighthearted now shall be my thoughts,
Jokes, smiles and stories will be sought.
This shall be brought by the power of three,
An it harm none, so mote it be.

Good Luck

Do not attempt to use this good luck spell in order to gain money, in case you get your wish in a way that might make you unhappy. Place the Wheel of Fortune and the Star Tarot cards face up on your altar, along with a dish of silver coins. Draw a four-leaf clover on a piece of paper and add it to your altar along with any numbers that you feel are lucky numbers.

When you have gathered your tools and everything is in place, cast your circle. When you are ready, stand or sit in front of your altar and recite this verse:

> Good luck be with me every day,
> Quirinus and Gamelia, hear me pray.
> Zadkiel bring me good news,
> Change my fortune that I may not lose.
> An it harm none, so mote it be.

Close your circle.

Good Results

For this spell start by decorating your altar with objects that are symbolic of information or calculation such as the High Priest card from the Tarot, the Rune symbol Ansuz, some leaves from an oak tree, a calculator or a key and nine pencils, pens or pieces of chalk. These items will add power to your intention.

When you have gathered your tools and everything is in place, cast your circle. When you are ready, stand or sit in front of your altar and recite this verse:

> Candles lit and prayers sent,
> With wishes full of good intent,
> A good result for all to see,
> An it harm none, so mote it be.

Close your circle.

Gratitude (to the Goddess)

Showing our gratitude to the Goddess balances out all the times we ask her for things. Lay a clean cloth on your altar. Choose objects that represent your gratitude to decorate your altar. These will be things that are very personal to you. When you have gathered your tools and everything is in place, cast a circle. When you are ready, stand or sit in front of your altar and thank the Goddess for all she has done for you or simply recite the verse below:

> I humbly thank the Goddess,
> For the gifts she has endowed.
> This prayer of thanks I offer up,
> With deep respect and head bowed,
> For bringing me what I desire,
> By the power of Water, Earth, Air and Fire.
> An it harm none so mote it be.

Close your circle.

Grief

We feel the heartbreak of grief most keenly when we lose someone close to us.

However, there are other situations involving loss when the emotion we experience is grief. For example, we can experience grief when a relationship breaks down, when there has been an irrevocable fallout with a friend or family member, when lifelong ambitions have been dashed without hope, when a job is lost (and with it sometimes a sense of identity) or a beloved pet dies. A friend recently experienced a broken relationship and was heartbroken by her situation. All who knew and loved her gathered to make a plea to the Goddess to help ease her emotional pain.

You, too, can do this if you have a friend whose heart is aching for any reason. Place a photograph of your friend on your altar together with an Apache teardrop crystal.

(There is a Native American story concerning the origin of this crystal's name that tells of some Native American warriors being attacked on a mountainside by US soldiers. The warriors who survived the attack bravely chose to jump over some cliffs to their deaths rather than surrender to the soldiers. The Great Spirit, Wakan Tanka, watched with horror as his people grieved for their lost warriors and such was his misery that as the mourners wept he turned their tears to Apache teardrop crystals. Some say that carrying an Apache teardrop crystal eases grief.)

When you have gathered your tools and everything is in place, cast a circle. When you are ready, stand or sit in front your altar. Recite whichever verse is appropriate for your purposes from those on the following two pages, then close your circle. (In the first verse, Lady Luna is the Moon but you can use Wakan Tanka if you prefer.)

To help another with grief over a broken relationship:

Lady Luna hear my plea,
Bless this child we bring to thee.
Dry all tears, and set emotions free,
This is our wish, this is our plea.
A relationship will have no life
If all it does is bring you strife.
If love returns to spread its glow,
True love enduring it should show.
Let none be harmed by this request,
To love, we strive to do our best.
Our sister's grief we here do mention,
Peace of mind is our intention.
So let her feel the love we share,
As astral sisters we do care.
We ask this wish by the power of three,
An harm none, so mote it be.

For another's grief:

> We ask for healing for your pain,
> Be assured it's not in vain.
> You ask, we hear, we understand,
> We offer you a loving hand.
> In prayer we join to ease your grief,
> We pray you will be given relief.
> An it harm none, so mote it be.

For your own grief:

> My heart it breaks, the loss is great.
> Dear Goddess help me through this pain
> That I may live my life again.
> Good memories and thoughts prevail,
> Hopelessness and grief curtailed.
> An it harm none, so mote it be.

Grounding

When you are meditating, you are elevated to a higher state of awareness and it is essential to ground yourself when you are finished. If you do not ground yourself, you are likely to be light-headed and unable to concentrate on mundane tasks. The simplest way to ground yourself is to make a cup of tea and eat something that has been formed in the ground such as root vegetables.

Sometimes we can feel like this without meditating. Again, eating root vegetables will help but you can also make use of an obsidian crystal. First prepare the crystal for this grounding spell by following the instructions on page 74 for crystal cleansing. Once cleansed, keep the obsidian crystal in your pocket and turn it over or handle it frequently. Doing this and reciting the verse opposite will help you to concentrate and keep your feet on the ground.

Crystal power come to me,
My feet keep on the ground.
For "airy-fairy" I'll not be,
While I have you around.
To think clearly is my intent,
To hear what's said is what is meant.
Decisions made and choices too,
This is what I ask of you.
An it harm none, so mote it be.

Guardian Angel

You can find your guardian angel by meditating.
Meditation can be hard to achieve at first. The aim
is to clear the mind, leaving it open to thinking new
thoughts or to transforming old thoughts into new,
calm positive ones. Persevere and with a little patience
and practice you can achieve the higher awareness
needed to find your guardian angel.

Start your meditation by relaxing in a comfortable
chair in front of which you have a lit candle. (Place the
candle on top of a plate on a coffee table or another
flat, stable surface.) You can play some relaxing music
but ensure it is not the kind of music that is going to
intrude into your thoughts.

Breathe deeply and slowly, relaxing your body, muscle
by muscle. Start at your toes. Clench them tightly
as you breathe in and relax them as you breathe out.
Do this with all your muscles from your toes to your
head.

When you are completely relaxed, gaze at the candle and try to see the different shapes created by its flame. Think about what these shapes represent. You may see figures or animals that mean something to you as you search for your guardian angel. When you feel comfortable doing this meditation, you can recite this verse before you start:

Guardian Angel come to me,
Listen to my heartfelt plea,
Let me see your shape appear,
Come to me, come close, come near.
Guide me, help me to understand,
Show me how to take your hand,
Lead me on my chosen way,
With these words, oh hear me pray.
An it harm none, so mote it be.

(See also "Grounding" on pages 112–13.)

Handfasting

A handfasting is a Pagan marriage ceremony that should take place in the summer months any time after the festival of Beltane (April 30th or May 1st). This simple ceremony can be carried out by anyone providing they are pure of heart. However, it is not legal unless it is carried out by a celebrant who is licensed to perform handfastings.

Many people choose to have a registry office wedding and then go somewhere special to have an unofficial handfasting ceremony. You can make a handfasting ceremony as elaborate or as simple as you like. In a simple ceremony, two people, somewhere outdoors, privately express their love and commitment to each other. In a more elaborate ceremony, there will be a High Priestess and, if available, a High Priest and they will share the responsibility of narrating the ceremony.

Here is a verse that can be used to express your love for your partner in a handfasting ceremony:

Here is a gift I give to you.
All that I have and all that I do,
Everything under heaven above,
I give to you, I give my love.
No word expressed with bad intent,
No deed to harm is ever meant.
This vow I make, I make to thee,
And ask it be blessed by the power of three.

Happiness

Here is a little happiness spell that you can chant
while you are doing your daily chores. It will help
you to get through your tasks and cheer you while
you work.

There is no need to cast a circle or prepare your altar
before you recite the following verse:

Happiness is what I seek,
Happiness to share.
For finding happy thoughts and deeds
I make this simple prayer.
I find it in the simplest things,
When the flowers grow, when the bird sings.
Happiness is all around,
For those that look it will be found.
An it harm none, so mote it be.

Happiness ~ For Another

This is a happiness spell that I prepared for one
of my friends who was having a difficult time. To
empower your spell you can take a small crystal
tumble stone (a stone polished by the tumbling
method) and dedicate it to your friend by holding
the stone in your dominant hand as you recite the
verse below. You don't have to cast a circle to do this
but it is nicer to do so.

My friend _____ means a lot to me
So I ask the Goddess, by the power of three,
Bring her joy, and bring her love
This is my plea to the lady above.
Let there be an end to any strife,
And bring sweet happiness to her life.
This is our wish, this is our plea,
An it harm none, so mote it be.

Healing ~ 1

The verse below can be used in a circle as a spell to send healing to anyone, anywhere, or it can simply be used as part of a morning prayer.

If you are going to work in circle, use green candles or a green cloth to decorate your altar. When you have gathered all your tools and everything is in place, cast a circle. When you are ready, stand or sit in front of your altar and recite this verse:

> To those in need may healing come
> Our prayers are sent as though we're one
> Be well, we bid the Goddess hear,
> Our friends and loved ones far or near.
> This is our wish, this is our plea,
> An it harm none, so mote it be.

Close your circle.

Healing ~ 2

The healing verse below can be used in a circle as a spell for a specific person (as described below) or recited as part of a prayer.

When you have gathered all your tools and everything is in place, cast a circle. When you are ready, stand or sit in front of your altar and recite the verse:

I ask for healing from above,
To bless _____ with light and love.
Bring good health this is my plea,
That she/he be well for all to see.
An it harm none, so mote it be.

Close your circle.

Hiding

There are days when you wish you could hide or suddenly become invisible. Maybe you cannot get a moment's peace at work because colleagues keep interrupting you or you might want to have a quiet day at home but you have neighbours who like to call in on a regular basis.

In Native American tradition, the fox is considered the symbol of invisibility. If you wish to become invisible, you can use the first verse on the next page with some help from your imagination.

Take some time before you begin your day to spread your arms out to your sides and imagine the spirit of the fox coming to you and draping a beautiful, rich copper-coloured fox coat over your shoulders.

Hold on to that image as you recite the following verse:

On my shoulders, little fox,
I wear your coat today.
Come one, come all,
For none will see me
While at work or play.
They walk right past me,
They pass and cannot see me.
Unseen I am content to be.
An it harm none, so mote it be.

When you are ready to be seen again, recite the
following:

I thank the spirit of the fox,
His coat he loaned to me,
My task is done and I am glad,
I return the gift by the power of three.
An it harm none, so mote it be.

Home ~ A Blessing

The following verse can be used as a blessing when you move into a new home or make changes around your existing home. Decorate your altar with the Rune symbol Othel and objects that are symbolic of your home such as your keys. When you have gathered your tools and everything is in place, cast your circle. Stand or sit in front of your altar and recite this verse:

> Blessed be our home and hearth,
> Our favourite place to be on earth.
> To us it is a perfect place,
> A happy and a homely space.
> We are happy and content,
> Our blessings are from heaven sent.
> Those who visit will agree,
> That we are blessed by the power of three.
> An it harm none, so mote it be.

Close your circle.

Imbolc

Imbolc (most commonly celebrated on February 2nd) is the festival dedicated to the Goddess Brigid. We celebrate Imbolc by spring-cleaning our houses from top to bottom and opening windows to welcome in the fresh new air. When the work is done, we light candles throughout the house to light the way for Spring. Witches decorate their altars with bright colours before casting their circles. Cast a circle then stand or sit in front of your altar and recite this verse:

> Light the candles, candles bright,
> The Goddess rises and brings the light.
> Clean the house and sweep, sweep, sweep,
> She rises from Her winter sleep.
> Snowdrops cheer Her on this day,
> Spring will soon be on its way.
> Light the candles with love so bright,
> And celebrate this Imbolc night.

Close your circle.

Imbolc ~ Blessing Seeds

For those of you who like to plant your own flowers, fruit or vegetables you can bless your seeds at Imbolc or when the Moon is full around the time of this festival. Here is a verse that you can use to bless your seeds at this time:

These seeds are ready to be grown,
And so I dig where they'll be sown.
The Lady watches while I work,
With rake and hoe and trowel and fork.
I ask these blessing for my seeds,
Keep them free from pests and weeds.
Please Lady find the heart to show,
Love for my seeds that they may grow.
An it harm none, so mote it be.

Inspiration

If you have a task to carry out and you cannot see what to do next, the best thing that you can do is walk away from task for a few moments. Sit quietly somewhere with your eyes closed and empty your head of all thoughts. After a few moments stand up, have a glass of water and return to what you were doing. Here is a verse that you can memorise and use whenever you cannot see the next step:

> May the light of inspiration
> Motivate and guide my way.
> May the Lord and Lady hear
> These sacred words I pray.
> Through this haze, I wish to feel
> Excitement for my task.
> To lift this cloud is my appeal,
> For inspiration is all I ask.
> An it harm none so mote it be.

Kindness ~ A Blessing

You can recite the verse below in a circle or write
down the words in a beautiful card and give it to the
person who has been kind to you. Decorate your altar
with objects such as photographs of friends, a dish of
sweets and some flowers. Cast your circle. Stand or sit
in front of your altar and recite this verse:

> You are kindness, this we know,
> For to others you always show
> Gentleness and acts of love,
> And this is seen from heaven above.
> May every blessing you bestow,
> Return to you but three times more.
> The Lady watches and she knows,
> The kindness you offer, she sees, it shows.
> Blessings for you from heaven sent,
> I send this wish with good intent.
> An it harm none, so mote it be.

Close your circle.

Kindness ~ A Request

There may be times when you feel sensitive and in need of a little TLC and yet those around you are being loud and insensitive, totally unaware of how you are feeling.

You should, of course, let them know how you're feeling but you can also say this little incantation to ask for kindness from whoever you meet:

Some calm I need today.
Cast meanness and anger away.
I'd like some stillness and some peace,
From stressfulness I need release.
Let everyone I meet this day,
Send kindly thoughts and words my way.
An it harm none, so mote it be.

Kindness ~ A Request

Lammas is the festival of the first harvest and it is held on August 1st. It is a time to give thanks for food such as breads and grains and seasonal fruits and vegetables.

We don't all have land on which to grow plants but even if you don't grow your own plants this can still be a time to show your gratitude for the seasonal foods that the Earth provides for us and that you can afford to purchase.

Decorate your altar with fruit and vegetables that you have grown, bread you have baked and home-made jams or jellies. Arrange your produce in baskets tied with coloured ribbons and use yellow or gold candles to show respect for the Sun God and green candles to show respect for Mother Earth.

When you have gathered your tools and everything is in place, cast a circle.

When you are ready, light your altar candles, then stand or sit in front of your altar and recite this verse:

We meet in love, give thanks and pray,
For Lammas crops and fruits this day.
Seeds sown become our food, our bread,
We think then of the winter ahead.
O Mother Earth be fruitful still,
Let future crops our larders fill.
We meet in love and gratitude,
For Summer's harvest of good food.

Close your circle.

Land to Buy

Use the verse opposite when you are trying to buy a piece of land. It can be used as part of a ritual in a circle or in the following manner.

Write out the verse and draw symbols around your text. The following Rune symbols are suitable: Othel representing the home, Sigel representing victory and Wunjo representing joy. You can also use Fehu representing wealth since you need wealth to purchase the land.

Place this picture of the verse in a frame and light a candle in front of it each day. Don't leave your candle unattended and when you put it out be sure to pinch or snuff it out, as blowing it out will scatter and weaken your wish.

Every time you look at your picture, read the verse and this will empower your intention.

A home to build is our desire,
Powers of Earth, Air, Water and Fire,
Grant our wish that we may be,
Keepers of this land we see.
A piece of earth to call our own
Would make our lives content.
By the power of three, let it be shown,
That we have good intent.
An it harm none, so mote it be.

Legal Issues

Fighting a legal case is a battle of nerves and wits which can drain your energy and your finances. Every bit of help is needed on these occasions.

The best day of the week to perform this ritual is a Wednesday. Decorate your altar by placing the Justice Tarot card face up on your altar together with the Rune symbol Tir (also known as Teiwaz). Place a heatproof dish on your altar in which is a layer of salt and a charcoal disc (the kind for incense burning.) Some crystals on your altar, such as jade, tiger's eye and turquoise, would be helpful.

You will also need some incense grains, herbs such as sage, some ground pepper, and some High John the Conqueror root (also known as jalap root or bindweed and not to be ingested).

When you have gathered your tools and everything is in place, cast your circle. Stand in front of your altar and light the charcoal disc (holding it with tweezers to do this). Place the disc back in the dish and when it is turning grey put the incense grains, herbs and root on top (but not the pepper).

Recite the following verse and as you reach the last line add a pinch of pepper to the dish to empower and speed up your intent:

> A legal battle we must win.
> Justice aid us, see their sin.
> Victory be ours to see,
> So that me and mine are free.
> Free from anger, free from strain,
> Free from this financial drain.
> Lessons they are meant to learn,
> Help us please, great Lord Herne.
> An it harm none, so mote it be.

Close your circle.

Litha ~ Summer Solstice

Litha (Midsummer or the Summer Solstice) falls on June 21st. This festival celebrates fertility and nature. The God and Goddess are at the height of their powers. It is also when we start to think of the harvest and Winter still to come. Litha is a good time for love and protection spells.

We celebrate this Sabbat in a circle. Brightly coloured ribbons or candles in reds and yellows can be used to decorate your altar. This is a verse that you could use in your circle:

> Lady and Lord this day is long,
> As night approaches, I worship thee.
> I offer up this little song,
> A rhyme of thanks, my prayer to thee.
> I humbly ask for your protection,
> And some time for honest reflection.
> My worship is both true and pure,
> My thanks I offer, to be sure.
> An it harm none, so mote it be.

Love Verse for a Partner

The first thing to remember is that you should never ask for someone in particular to be your partner because you could end up in a damaging relationship and find it difficult, if not impossible, to get out of it. This verse is worded for someone in an existing, committed relationship. It can be written down and framed for your partner.

You're my love, the one for me,
And may you always loving be.
I hope your dreams may all come true,
This is my wish from me to you.
These blessings, may the Goddess send,
May past problems come to an end.
Wishes granted in the coming years,
Of this I'm sure the Goddess hears.
My love, as always, true will be,
Blessed by the power of three.
An it harm none, so mote it be.

Love Ritual Verse

Remember that you must never ask for someone in particular to be your partner in a love spell as this would be interfering with another's will. However, you can say that you are ready for love in general to come into your life.

You can use this verse in your love ritual:

My heart is empty, no-one to love,
Lady bless me from above.
Let me love me, then love I give,
Show me love and how to live.
I'm ready now for love to come,
And when it does we think as one.
A perfect match this love will be,
Blessed by the power of three.
An it harm none, so mote it be.

Love in Winter

One day I passed an art gallery and was very taken by a picture I saw in the window of a loving couple wrapped up in their Winter clothes and each other as they walked along. I could see someone I knew and cared for in that picture. Suddenly this verse came to me. So I bought the picture, typed out the verse and sent it to my friend. Use this verse to ask love to find someone you care for:

Summer leaves begin to go,
And Autumn winds begin to blow.
A heavy heart will soon be light,
As love comes into Winter bright.
True love will find you, you will know
Nice to share during Winter snow.
In love fulfilled you soon will be,
Blessed by the power of three.
This is my wish, this is my plea,
An it harm none, so mote it be.

Mabon

Mabon (the Autumn equinox) heralds the end of
Summer. It takes place on September 21st, 22nd or
23rd. Witches celebrate and give thanks in a circle
for the last harvest before Winter. Their celebrations
might include bread and wine. It is a good time for
spells that ask for harmony and balance. Decorate
your altar as described on page 130 for Lammas.
Cast your circle. When you are ready, stand or sit in
front of your altar and and recite the following verse:

> The Maiden's time has come and gone,
> And soon she'll be a Mother,
> And then the Holy King will reign,
> And we'll celebrate together.
> We rest this land that we do tend,
> For Spring will come again,
> And all that's broken we will mend,
> And plant our seeds and grain.

Close your circle.

Money

For this spell, decorate your altar with coins and items symbolic of wealth (actual objects or photographs). Crystals are considered to depict wealth and citrine in particular attracts money.

When you have gathered your tools and everything is in place, cast your circle. When you are ready, stand or sit in front of your altar and recite the following verse:

> Money comes to me to be,
> Well off and safe and worry free.
> Our lives are blessed for all to see.
> These wishes come by the power of three,
> An it harm none, so mote it be.

Close your circle. Keep a copy of the verse in your purse or wallet.

Miscarriage

It is very sad when a baby is lost because of a miscarriage and both parents can grieve for a long time. For friends and family it can be difficult to know what to say to the grieving mother or father. The verse below can be written in a card and given to the parents along with a piece of Apache teardrop crystal to help ease their pain.

Little baby, we will weep,
While in the Goddess's arms you sleep.
When the grieving has been done,
Your time to live again will come.
Mother, father, little one,
The goddess watches over you all as one.
My prayer I send, your hearts to heal,
All things are part of life's great wheel.
And though today it is hard to see,
You will be blessed by the power of three.
An it harm none, so mote it be.

New Year Blessing

Samhain (Halloween) is the Pagan New Year. This festival is held on October 31st and the Celtic Wheel of the Year starts on this date.

The verse below can be sent with good wishes to a loved one at this time of year and on January 1st in the conventional calendar:

> This New Year blessing comes to say,
> May good wishes come your way.
> It's sent with love from me to you,
> To thank you for the work you do.
> May the Goddess bless your way,
> As you work and as you play.
> Blessed by the power of three,
> This is my wish so mote it be.

Ostara

Ostara (Easter) falls on or around March 20th at the time of the Spring equinox. This festival honours the richness and wealth that Mother Nature has brought to humans. Celebrate this festival in a circle. First decorate your altar with coloured hard-boiled eggs, yellow candles, spring flowers and some of the seeds blessed during Imbolc. Cast your circle, then stand or sit in front of your altar and recite this verse:

Ostara comes but once a year,
And with it comes the Spring,
A time to plant and spread good cheer,
A time to dance and sing.
But this year with the Moon so close,
Its powers we should employ
To think of others not so blessed,
To send them love and joy,
An it harm none, so mote it be.

Close your circle.

Passion

While you cannot ask for a specific person to come into your life, you can ask for more passion in general.

Before you begin this ritual, take a warm, relaxing bath to which you have added patchouli or ylang-ylang essential oil. Relax and focus on your intention. Do not pull out the plug before you get out of the bath. Once you are out and dried, put on a red gown or robe.

Decorate your altar with a red cloth, a piece of emerald, sapphire or ruby jewellery and add some things made of copper or brass. Place one white and one red candle on the altar with a vase of poppies or tiger lilies (or any other red flowers if these are hard to find).

When you have gathered all your tools and everything is in place, cast your circle.

When you are ready, stand or sit in front of your altar and recite this verse:

> Passion burns within my loins,
> My heart, my soul afire.
> Lillith bring to me this night,
> The passion I desire.
> An it harm none, so mote it be

Close your circle.

Passing Over

It is very hard to come to terms with the death of a loved one but the following ritual may be of some comfort (see also "Grief" on page 108).

First prepare your altar. Take a potted rosemary plant and place it on your altar along with a piece of paper on which you have written the verse on the following page (or a verse of your own composing). Place a piece of blank paper and a pen on the altar as well. Decorate your altar with a photograph of the person who has passed over and things that were special to them such as a piece of jewellery.

When you have gathered your tools and everything is in place, cast your circle. Sit at your altar. On the piece of blank paper write a letter to your loved one saying everything that you regret not saying to them in life. It is fine to have a moment's anger or to cry while you are writing this letter – both are part of the grieving process.

Take your letter and fold it up very small. Remove the rosemary plant from its pot and place the letter at the bottom of the pot. Return the rosemary to the pot and pour some water over it. Now recite the following verse:

_____ is embraced in love,
In the arms of the Lady above.
Rest in peace and love we say,
While in our hearts you'll always stay.
One day to come you will return, the Goddess tells us so.
Until that time, our duty is to love and let you go,
But this is hard and makes us grieve,
Of this I'm sure you know,
Our hearts are sore you had to leave,
But it was your time to go.
An it harm none, so mote it be.

Close your circle.

Peace

This is a verse that asks for peace. It can be said as part of a morning ritual or prayer, especially if you have a family member in the armed forces.

Let peace be felt upon the land,
No weapons lifted by any hand.
May farmers prosper as animals graze,
And Pax be with us to hear our praise.
No wars to fight or arms to bear,
And all we have we try to share.
To love is better than to fight,
This is our prayer both morn and night.
The Goddess she doth hear our plea,
An it harm none, so mote it be.

Peace of Mind

This ritual can be performed to help someone who is stressed and anxious. Decorate your altar using flowers or candles that are dark blue, violet or purple. Keep it free from any clutter.

When you have gathered your tools and everything is in place, cast your circle. When you are ready, stand or sit in front of your altar and recite this verse:

Be calm my child, the Lady says,
Healing comes in many ways.
For you will settle body and mind,
And peace I'm sure you soon will find.
This blessing comes with good intent,
Healing for you has now been sent.
An it harm none, so mote it be.

Close your circle.

Pregnancy

The news of a friend or family member's pregnancy brings much joy and everyone wants to share in the celebration and express their good wishes.

Here is a verse that you can write on a greetings card to show that you too are happy about the news of the new child that is going to be born.

A baby coming is a joy,
Whether it be a girl or a boy.
Good wishes sent, good wishes meant.
This is my wish, 'tis my intent
May mother and child blessed be,
By the Goddess and the power of three.
An it harm none, so mote it be.

Problems

You can use this ritual to help get rid of any problems you may have.

 First place on your altar some seeds (sunflowers grow quickly and are ideal for this task), a flowerpot, some soil, water, a sheet of paper and a pen. Then, when you have gathered your tools and everything is in place, cast your circle.

When you are ready, sit in front of your altar and write down on the sheet of paper a list of all the problems that are affecting your life. Put the finished list at the bottom of the flowerpot, fill it with soil, add your seeds then cover them with a little more soil.

Water your pot, then stand it in front of your altar and recite the verse that follows:

Problems in the past I had,
So many did I know.
But now I bury all the bad
And ask the seeds to grow.
And as they grow they feed upon
What I no longer want.
My problems now they will be gone
As seed becomes a plant.
Grow for me and flower too,
My problems now are gone.
This coming year will be so good,
As problems, I have none.
An it harm none, so mote it be.

Close your circle. Be sure to care for your growing plants because neglecting them will delay the resolution of your problems.

Property to Buy

When you have seen a property that you would like to buy, cut out a picture of the property (from the estate agent's schedule or a newspaper advertisement) and write "Sold to (your name)" across the front of it. Place the picture in a frame with an old key (or a picture of a key) under the glass. Then sit it in a prominent place in your home.

Light a candle in front of the framed picture daily. If you have to put it out, pinch it or use a candle snuffer. Do not blow it out as you will scatter your wishes.

Print out or write down the verse opposite and lay this in front of your framed picture. Each time you look at the picture, recite the verse. You can adapt the verse to reflect the features of the house that are important to you. Insert the name (or number and street) of the house that you want to buy at the beginning of the verse.

_____ is the address we see
As a place for our family to happily be.
I ask the Goddess to secure this home,
   That we may make it as our own.
   A school nearby and a garden too,
   A park to enjoy under skies so blue,
Where we can relax and share our love,
   A gift from the Goddess high above.
   An it harm none, so mote it be.

Property to Rent

Follow the instructions given under "Property to Buy"
but use the following verse for property to rent:

With Fire and Light I bring to life,
Intentions honest, free from strife.
By candlelight I make my vow,
The time for us to move is now.
No more delays to circumvent,
We see the home we wish to rent.
A home that's filled with joy and peace,
Blessed with love above and beneath.
It is our will for all to see,
An it harm none, so mote it be.

Property to Sell

Follow the instructions under "Property to Buy" but use the following verse for property to sell. If you have a partner, insert his or her name in the space provided.

My property I have to sell,
Once done, our finances will be well.
I ask the powers that they be,
Benevolent to _____ and me,
And then will come a buyer who
Will make an offer that is true.
And, funds in place, we will say "Yes",
For we are blessed by the great God Bes.
An it harm none, so mote it be.

Property to Share

Finding a suitable roommate or person with whom to share a flat or home can be difficult, but this verse may help you. It can be performed as part of a ritual in a circle or it can be written down and framed and placed on a shelf with a candle lit daily in front of it.

A friend to share my home I seek,
Let one who comes be kind and neat,
And pay their share when it is due,
And have interests similar too.
Let no anger between us pass,
Let no strife nor quarrels last,
Let there be friendship for us to share,
Let there be kindness to show we care.
And in our home let blessings be,
That come to us from Goddesses three,
This is my wish, this is my plea,
An it harm none, so mote it be.

Protection ~ From Threat

In the tradition of the Old Ways we do not harm others, but if someone is threatening you, it is acceptable to return whatever they are sending you. Put photographs of soldiers or knights and some turquoise stones or jewellery on your altar. Place a mirror in the centre, angled so that there appear to be twice as many objects.

Cast a circle. Stand in front of your altar with your elbows bent and the back of your hands under your chin. Recite the following verse and as you say "Back to you I send your harm" push your hands outwards as though you were sending back the threatening energy:

Under threat, you think I am, but a victim I am not.
Back to you I send your harm, for I have not forgot,
The Lady watches over me, each and every day,
Returns your evil deeds to you, lest harm
should come my way.
This is my wish, my prayer too, your evil
ways return to you.
So mote it be.

Close your circle.

The verse below can also be used as a spell in a ritual:

You cast on us your evil eye, and this we
now return.
Your evil deeds will catch you up and
soon the time will come,
For those who suffered at your hand to
unite and act as one.
Be gone, we cry, and leave this place in
harmony and peace.
Be gone, we cry, with your evil eye and let
the problems cease.
We send back what you put out, and
certain you can see,
The Goddess she empowers us and brings
the power of three.
So mote it be.

Protection ~ Of Your Home

If you feel insecure for any reason, this is an ideal spell to protect yourself and your home.

Search around your home – in drawers, toolboxes, in the garden shed or garage – for all the rusty nails, bent pins and screws that you can find.

Place them in a jar with a lid. Write the first of the verses that follow on page 162 on a piece of paper. Place the written verse in the same jar as the nails, put the lid on and bury the jar outside, near your front door.

If you do not have anywhere to bury the jar, you can put some rusty nails, etc, and the written verse into a smaller jar instead (such as an empty moisturiser container) and plant it in a flowerpot just inside your front door.

If you also have a back door, use two jars so that you are protected at each side of your home.

A spell for protecting your home:

> Little bottle full of pins,
> Sharp and jagged edges,
> Keep away the one who sins,
> From our boundaries and hedges.
> Keep us well and keep us warm,
> Watch o'er us when we're sleeping.
> Keep us safe and free from harm,
> And always in your keeping.
> An it harm none, so mote it be.

A spell for protecting your family:

> Lord and Lady high above,
> From us send any harm away,
> Protect us now in light and love,
> Keep us safe both night and day.
> An it harm none, so mote it be.

Protection ~ From Jealousy

Often people who display negative energy towards you are jealous of you. Jealousy is a very disruptive energy. If you find yourself a victim of someone's jealousy, carry a piece of turquoise or wear turquoise clothes or accessories for protection. The spell below will also help to protect you.

Start by placing the following on your altar: a picture of the "Eye of Horus" (for protection, see page 19), several turquoise stones and turquoise or blue candles. Cast your circle then, when you are ready, recite this verse:

> Protect me, for jealousy has come my way.
> From the evil eye, guard me every day.
> Wadjet keep me free from harm,
> 'Tis why I say this blessed charm.
> Goddess of protection high above,
> Surround me now with all your love.
> This is my wish, this is my plea,
> An it harm none, so mote it be.

Purification ~ Consecrated Water

Consecrated water can be used for many purposes such as cleansing tools, working in a circle, blessing your home or eliminating night terrors or bad dreams.

Follow these instructions to prepare consecrated water. You will need a bowl of water and some salt. Stand by a window when the Moon is full or waxing (rising). Put three pinches of salt into the bowl of water, then raise your dominant hand and point at the Moon. Imagine that you are drawing energy from the Moon into your hand. Place your pointed finger into the bowl of salted water and stir three times while repeating the words below:

> Salt is life, here is life, sacred be without strife.
> Salt is life, here is life, sacred be without strife.
> Salt is life, here is life, blessed be without strife.

You can use this consecrated water immediately or you can bottle it and label it for future use.

Purification ~ For Yourself

To purify yourself, follow the instructions below.

Fill a bath with water, place four lit candles at each corner of your bath. Pour a cup of rock or sea salt into the bath water in the shape of a figure of eight and as you do so recite these words:

> Salt is life, here is life, sacred be without strife.
> Salt is life, here is life, sacred be without strife.
> Salt is life, here is life, blessed be without strife.

Step into your bath, lie back and relax.

You can have some music playing in the background or silence if you prefer.

While you are in your bath, visualise that mind, body and spirit are being cleansed and purified.

Do not remove the plug until you are out of the bath.

When you have stepped out of your bath, remove the plug then stand and watch the water flowing away. As you do so, imagine any negative energy you may have flowing away from you.

When this is done, you can dress to perform a ritual, get ready to go out or get ready to go to bed.

Purification ~ For Your Wiccan Tools

Place any tools, jewellery or other items that you wish to cleanse on or next to your altar. When you have gathered your tools and everything is in place, cast your circle. Using consecrated water, sprinkle those items that you wish to cleanse and protect while reciting the following verse several times:

Bless it clean, bless it pure,
Make its purpose true and sure.
Vibrations dark I send away,
Keep pure and light from this day.
Blessings come from high above,
Blessings that are filled with love.
With Water, Earth, Air and Fire,
This is my wish, this my desire.
An it harm none, so mote it be.

Close your circle.

Recalling Dreams

Crystals are useful when it comes to recalling dreams, particularly amethyst, clear quartz, and rutilated quartz. Once a month, take your chosen crystal and wash it in running water (when the Moon is full), then dedicate it to recalling your dreams by holding it in your hand and reciting the following verse:

I dedicate this crystal,
To unfold my dream to me.
And if that dream is happy,
Reveal it all to me.
But if it's dark then banish it,
For I do not wish to see.
An it harm none, so mote it be.

Place the crystal under your pillow and keep a notepad and pen by your bed so that you can write down the details of your dreams when you wake.

Restful Sleep ~ For Another

Prepare a small pouch containing some lavender flowers (or infuse it with lavender essential oil of). Add an amethyst crystal to the pouch and a piece of paper on which you have written the following verse:

To sleep, sweet dreams I wish for you,
That you may sleep with a peace that's true.
Rest, without a care,
Sleep without despair.
I ask the Goddess to enfold
You in her warm embrace.
And in her arms you will behold,
Her benevolence and grace.
An it harm none, so mote it be.

Tie up the pouch with a purple ribbon and give it to the person who needs to have a good night's undisturbed sleep.

Restful Sleep ~ For Yourself

Ensure there are clean sheets on your bed and that your room is neat and tidy. Prepare a small pouch containing some lavender flowers and an amethyst crystal. Tie it up with a purple ribbon and place it under your pillow. Take a purifying bath (as shown in "Purification for yourself" on pages 165–6) and then put on clean nightclothes.

As you lie in bed, quietly and respectfully repeat these words to yourself, out loud if you wish, until you fall asleep:

> Goddess honour me with rest,
> To sleep calm and sound is my request.
> Let me quickly fall asleep,
> In a slumber that is sweet and deep.
> When I awake, refreshed I'll be,
> I ask this by the power of three.
> An it harm none, so mote it be.

Reunion ~ Friends

Decorate your altar with symbols of happy times that you have shared with your friend such as photographs and letters. Place the High Priestess, the Hermit and the Six of Cups Tarot cards face up on your altar and nine lit candles in a row. Cast your circle. Stand or sit in front of your altar and recite the following verse:

> To see my friend _____ and share the past,
> The present and the future,
> Is my request. Let's share again
> Good memories and good humour.
> Give us the chance to reunite,
> Let the path to each other come to light.
> The Lady listens to my plea,
> Let us be blessed by the power of three,
> An it harm none, so mote it be.

Close your circle.

Samhain

Samhain (pronounced *sow-en* and also known as Halloween) takes place on October 31st. It is a special time for followers of the Old Ways.

At this time of the year we honour our ancestors and loved ones who have departed in our lifetime by laying an extra place at our dinner table for them.

Before you begin this ritual, prepare the food that you will eat and lay your table for any guest that you will invite, remembering to lay an extra place in honour of those who have passed over.

When all of that is done, decorate your altar using a black cloth and black candles. Display photos of loved ones who have passed. When everything is in place, cast your circle, light your altar candles and when you are ready recite the verse opposite:

All is well, the veil is thin, our loved ones
gone are near.
We call to them tonight "come in" and this
Samhain they will hear.
We remember those passed over and set
their place at table.
Welcome one and welcome all, return if
you are able.
We ask of you to guide our path, wherever
we do walk.
Though you are on another plane, you bide
within our hearts.
When day is done and dawn it breaks and
the veil begins to grow,
Our hearts still feel the same. Our love
remains to show.
We will remember loved ones dear, this and
every other year.
The things we shared, the love we felt, of
that we can be sure.
An it harm none, so mote it be.

Close your circle.

Scrying

Scrying is looking for visions of the past, present or future by gazing into a reflective surface. Often this is done using a crystal ball or in a scrying mirror (a black mirror) but any smooth reflective surface will do. You are looking with your "mind's eye" rather than looking for actual reflections.

It's easy to make your own scrying mirror by using the bevelled glass from an old clock face and painting the inside of the face black, or lay the clock face in a box that is slightly bigger than the glass and lined with black cloth.

Scrying should be done in a circle and it needs practice. Gaze into your glass every day and let your mind allow itself to see visions and shapes.

Cast a circle where you will be working and light a candle by the scrying glass. Recite the verse below.

Guiding Spirit from above,
Come to me with light and love.
Imbue my mirror, o mighty Seer,
With visions I might see and hear.
And from it guidance I can give,
To follow truly as I live.
No harm will come to those who ask
For visions from this scrying glass.
Let it be done in truth and love,
Empowered with blessing from above.
This is my will, this is my plea
An it harm none, so mote it be.

Close your circle.

Secrets

When someone shares a secret with you, or if you have one of your own, it can be difficult to stop yourself revealing it. While you are trying to keep a secret, avoid things to do with the number five and stay close to the number two (the number two depicts secrets but the number five reveals them). Recite the verse below any time you feel the urge to share a secret. If you decide to work in a circle to avoid revealing your secret, everything on your altar should be in pairs. Use the High Priestess Tarot card (face up) and the Rune symbol Peorth on your altar.

In my heart I hold the key,
To the secret none should see.
Never will it be revealed,
My intention pure, my lips are sealed.
Blessed by the power of three,
An it harm none, so mote it be.

Sobriety

The only person who can stop someone drinking is the person who is drinking to excess. However, there are a few things that may help. The person who drinks too much should carry a piece of amethyst, which is said to have properties that aid sobriety. I have also found that people drink less and sometimes stop altogether after Reiki treatments or after taking a course to learn about Reiki. Here is a verse you can write out and give to the person who overindulges. They should fold it up and put it inside their shoe.

> I ask the Lord and Lady please,
> Take this burden, help to ease
> This habit that's destroying me.
> Help me please and set me free.
> I ask this by the power of three,
> An it harm none, so mote it be.

Spirit Guidance

When you are looking for guidance from above, use the verse opposite in a circle.

Decorate your altar with things that depict spiritual guides. These can be photographs or statues of animals such as an eagle, a wolf or a dolphin or any other animal that is relevant to you.

You can also use photographs or statues of Gods or Goddesses or any other spiritual figures that you like.

The colours purple, violet and dark blue are appropriate and you can use these colours for an altar cloth and candles. Crystals are also helpful and you can scatter some around your altar.

When you are ready and your circle is cast, recite the following verse:

Wise ones, elders, come show me how.
Angels, loved ones guide me now.
This portal will allow you entry,
If you can pass the guardian sentry.
Your humble being waits below.
Teach me, show me, that I may know,
The wisdom given from above,
That comes to me with light and love.
An it harm none, so mote it be.

Close your circle.

Success

Success is something that we have to work hard for, but a little spell never hurts. Here is a verse that can be used in rituals or it can be framed and displayed where you will see it often:

Success may come and it may go,
The wheel it ever turns.
But we have learned through efforts true
Work hard and we will earn.
For efforts made, rewards we reap,
The Lady blesses us.
She grants to us, our bounty keep.
Her love to us she shows.
We will succeed in all we do,
With effort, skill and kindness too.
Our lives are blessed for all to see,
These wishes come within a three.
An it harm none, so mote it be.

Travel

If you have a journey to make, dedicate this verse to Desna, the Goddess of travel. When your tools are gathered and everything is ready, cast a circle. Stand or sit in front of your altar and recite this verse:

> Desna, Desna hear me pray
> Keep my road safe night and day.
> Oh Goddess of the travelling kind,
> Keep me sound in body and mind.
> Desna, Desna you're the guide
> Of travellers far and wide.
> Goddess Desna, my thanks to you
> For safe passage and path true.
> An it harm none, so mote it be.

Close your circle. Why not print out a copy of this and keep it in your car or with your travel documents.

Troubled Times ~ For Another

This is a verse that you can use in a circle to help someone who is enduring a difficult time and needs your support. Decorate your altar with objects that suggest tranquillity. Blues and violets are shades that are useful. Also include a photograph of the person that you are praying for or simply write their name on a piece of paper and lay it on the centre of your altar. Cast your circle. Recite the following verse:

Prayers needed, prayers sent,
Healing and loving is the intent.
A troubled time the strength to bear,
The Goddess listens and hears our prayer.
May these troubles be of the past,
May our prayers last and last,
Peace be on your troubled soul,
This is my wish, this is my goal.
An it harm none, so mote it be.

Close your circle.

Troubled Times ~ For Yourself

Decorate your altar using white as the main colour
and keep it uncluttered. Cast a circle. Give thanks to
the Lord and Lady for the gifts you have already been
given and ask for help to end your current difficulties.
Recite this verse:

My tears are spent, I cry no more,
The Lady makes it so.
The wheel has turned of that I'm sure
Her blessings soon I'll know.
I've had my share of lessons now,
And from them I have learned,
The Lady doth her gifts bestow,
Through times of tears we've earned.
My smiles return and I am glad,
The difficulties have passed,
Though it was hard and sometimes bad,
My joy returns at last.
An it harm none, so mote it be.

Close your circle.

Visualization

Visualising is like imagining, only better, as it should involve all the senses (not just our sight) to make whatever we are visualising feel real. Witches need to be able to visualise the outcome of a spell in all its aspects and in a positive way if the spell is to succeed. One way to start practising visualisation is by focusing your attention on the space between your eyes. Do this when you are very relaxed and with your eyes closed. At first, you will see nothing but don't be alarmed if one day you see an eye. This is our so-called "third eye" whose primary function is seeing beyond our physical world. It allows us to see beyond time and space in the form of visions and images. It gives us the ability to clearly imagine and visualise the positive future which we desire. Try to look through the eye rather than at the eye and soon

pictures will begin to form. These may be random images and you may not understand what they mean initially, but just go with the flow and eventually you will understand what they are saying and be able to put them to good use through your own mental processes. Here is a verse that you can recite before you perform this exercise:

I close my eyes that I may see,
Pictures that are sent to me,
To understand what they imply,
I seek to know, I seek to try.
Lady show me, tell me so,
What I see that I should know.
And when I see, I know what's true,
This is the gift I ask from you,
An it harm none, so mote it be.

Victory

When you are trying to win at something, memorise this verse and place a copy of it in your shoe. Every time you feel it under your foot, recite the verse and this will remind you to continue trying to achieve your goal. You can also use the verse as a spell in a circle after decorating your altar with the following: objects that are typical of a victory; the Six of Wands (depicting triumph) and Wheel (bringing luck) Tarot cards; and small trophies or photographs of trophies (empowering your intent).

> Burning flame that burns so true,
> Bring to me a victory too.
> Make me strong both day and night,
> To meet this challenge with my might.
> Victory it shall be mine,
> Blessed be the powers that shine.
> An it harm none, so mote it be.

Wiccan Rede ~ by Soraya

The Wiccan Rede is a brief guide to the practice of
Wicca, showing honour and respect to the Goddess.
This is a version that I created.

Follow me in perfect love, in honour,
truth and perfect trust.
Abide my laws in every day. Be true
to me in every way.
My circle cast for all to see, let none enter
who should not be.
Around I go times one, two, three;
full moon above it watches me.
Deosil the circle cast, rituals set — true to last.
But in the dark to banish all,
Widdershins it is my call.
By Lady's light, I heed the rule,
and do no harm by any tool.
I do to you as you to me, lest bad
return to me by three.
These words the Wiccan rede fulfil,
An it harm none, do as you will.

Wishes

Here is a ritual that you can perform for a wish to come true. Take pen and paper and write down your wish expressing it as if it has already happened. For example, if your wish was for a new or better car you would write the following: "I have a new car now, no harm came to me or mine in the process and I am happy that my car is safe and reliable."

It is written in this way first to empower it as though it has actually happened and second, which is more important, your car will come to you for a good reason and not because you have been involved in an accident.

You should always be careful how you ask for things, as you may get your wish but not in the manner that you expected. Remember if you are asking for love, do not name a specific person because that interferes

with their destiny and you may find that you end up trapped in an unhappy relationship. Instead, ask for love that can be returned to come to you.

Place your written wish in a red envelope, then cast your circle in your usual fashion. Recite the verse on page 190 to the Lord and Lady, holding your red envelope between the palms of your hands while doing so. When you are finished, close your circle.

Take your letter to some running water such as river or the sea (if the latter, make sure the tide is going out otherwise your letter will come back to you and your wish will not come true). Stand on the river bank or on the shoreline, repeat the verse, express your wish and throw your letter onto the water.

A heartfelt wish I ask of you
That's made with good intent.
Lord and Lady I honour you,
No harm from me is meant.
I wish that _____.
This wish is good and true.
May the Goddess aid me with my wish,
May she guide my hand anew.
Let no bad come from granting my plea,
An it harm none, so mote it be.

To grant a wish for another person, give him or her a red envelope and tell them to write out their wish and place it in the envelope. Reword the verse to name your friend and to accomodate whether they want their wish to remain secret. Then they can take the envelope to running water or you can do that for them.

Yule Verse

Yule is the pagan midwinter festival, celebrated on December 21st or 22nd (the Winter Solstice). It is the shortest day and longest night of the year. At this Sabbat, we honour the birth of the new king.

The King is born. We hear the call:
"Come celebrate, come one, come all."
The old King died to pave the way,
And yet he has returned this day.
Come celebrate the wheel of life.
Come celebrate, forget the strife.
'Tis time for cheer, 'tis time to love.
Give thanks for blessings from above.
Friends and family gather round,
Listen for the angels' sound.
Celebrate our Sun God new,
For He hath come for me and you.
So mote it be.

Published 2019 by Geddes & Grosset, an imprint of
The Gresham Publishing Company Ltd, Academy Park,
Building 4000, Gower Street, Glasgow, G51 1PR, Scotland.

First published in hardback, 2015 as
The Little Book of Spells ISBN 978-1-84205-873-2

Page decoration © Andriy Zholudyev, courtesy of Shutterstock

ISBN 978-1-85534-044-2

Printed and bound in the EU